Day-to-Day Discipline
That Works With Teenagers

By Ann B. Cannon

Family
Tree™

Group®

Loveland, Colorado

Day-to-Day Discipline That Works With Teenagers

Copyright © 1990 by Ann B. Cannon

First Printing

Credits

Edited by Lee Sparks
Designed by Jill Bendykowski
Cover design by Judy Atwood Bienick
Illustrations by Aaron Bacall

Scripture quotations are from the Holy Bible, New International Version. Copyright © 1973, 1978, 1984 International Bible Society. Used by permission of Zondervan Bible Publishers.

Library of Congress Cataloging-in-Publication Data

Cannon, Ann.
    Day-to-day discipline that works with teenagers / by Ann B. Cannon.
        p.   cm. — (Fast help for parents)
    ISBN 1-55945-011-8
    1. Family—Religious life. 2. Parenting—Religious aspects—Christianity. 3. Discipline of children—United States. 4. Teenagers—United States—Attitudes. 5. Adolescence. I. Title. II. Series.
BV4526.2.C265   1990
248.8'45—dc20
                                      90-35029
                                        CIP

Printed in the United States of America

Dedication

To Corey and Casey, who provided so many opportunities
for me to learn creative discipline, and didn't give up even
though I was a slow learner.

Acknowledgments

I'm ever grateful to the numerous parents and teenagers who
shared their personal failures and successes in discipline. Their
experiences shaped my patterns of discipline.

With appreciation to Jeana Fortenberry—my youth minister
and caring friend—who loaned me her library and offered ideas
when I got stuck, and who still listens to my latest discipline
struggle.

Warmest thanks to Eugene C. Roehlkepartain, who asked me
to do this book, offered excellent guidance throughout the
project, started out as editor and ended up as friend. A special
thanks to Lee Sparks, who worked on the final copy and helped
it all make sense. Blessings!

CONTENTS

CHAPTER**ONE**

THE DISCIPLINE DILEMMA

❖

"**T**hree months ago I was a rational, sane adult—capable of making decisions, confident in what I believed was right and wrong. Today I'm a babbling idiot. I can't speak a single sentence my child understands. I can't control her. And I'm completely confused about what's right or wrong."

She sat before me disabled and distraught, no longer the competent person I'd known. What had happened? Nothing much, except her darling daughter had become a teenager. Suddenly my friend's discipline methods no longer worked.

"Last night I told Susie it was time to get off the phone," my friend continued, her eyes begging for support. "After all, isn't an hour long enough? With a raised eyebrow Susie hissed, 'This conversation is important. Don't you know that?' "

She shook her head slowly, as if to clear up her confusion. "I don't think I'm doing a very good job of parenting," she concluded sadly. "Understanding teenagers isn't easy."

In one way my friend is wrong: She's doing a better-than-she-thinks job of launching her teenage daughter into adulthood. On the other hand, she's right: Understanding teenagers isn't easy. And disciplining them is even more difficult. It takes lots of time, energy, prayer and communication.

But often, things just don't work out, work well or work at all. How do we as parents of adolescents apply discipline in ways that help our soon-to-be-adults learn responsibility? And how can we still remain in control of our homes? That's the discipline dilemma we'll look at in this chapter.

UNDERSTANDING CREATIVE DISCIPLINE

When our children were younger, discipline was simple. We took away a toy, sent them to their rooms or forbade them to play with unacceptable playmates. We restricted their world.

Then they became teenagers and the rules changed. We no longer totally controlled their world. Yet they lacked the skills and maturity to control their own world. Somewhere between total control and no control, we search for a magic formula to turn self-centered, chaotic children into sane, sensible adults. That formula begins with effective, creative discipline. Here's how it works:

● *Creative discipline adjusts to each child's unique-nesses.* Negative discipline remains rigid, using a set discipline method for every situation.

Our son, Corey, prefers choices to an unsupported no. He thinks through problems. We disciplined him best by asking him to think about a particular situation and by suggesting choices.

Although his sister Casey needs to know the "why," she's more willing to accept yes or no responses. Too many choices frustrate her.

● *Creative discipline lets the punishment fit the crime.* Negative discipline punishes to pay back for misbehavior. Negative discipline can also produce overkill.

When Corey returned the car with no gas, we gave him a choice—either pay us for the gasoline he used, or don't drive the car for two days. He chose the latter. He still kept up his regular activities. But without a car he had to scramble to find rides.

Grounding him would've been negative discipline. He wouldn't need a car if he couldn't leave the house, so he wouldn't miss its use.

● *Creative discipline also looks for creative ways to discipline rather than punish.* During the summer following his ninth grade, Corey announced that he couldn't help me clean the house because he was on vacation. He rambled on about how he deserved time to do what he wanted to do.

So I took a vacation too. I didn't wash Corey's clothes. I didn't fix Corey's meals. I didn't chauffeur Corey around. Corey soon saw that some responsibilities don't take vacations.

● *Creative discipline not only seeks to modify or*

change inappropriate behavior, but it also teaches new behavior. Today I made Casey's bed, something I don't normally do unless she asks. She was running late for school, and I knew she'd asked a friend over after school. I made her bed and picked up her room as an act of love and concern for her busy schedule.

Casey is just as likely to help me in unexpected ways. Sometimes I return from a trip to find she's done the laundry. I treat Casey with courtesy, showing her I care. She's learning to return the courtesy.

● *Creative discipline affirms as well as instructs.* Negative discipline remains focused on irresponsible, unacceptable behavior. Rather than pointing out a teenager's shortcomings, creative discipline looks for one good trait to praise. Praise is a highly effective motivator.

The past six weeks haven't been good for Casey's grades. She knew it, and she warned me that her report card would be bad. And the grades were. But the comments from teachers were positive.

So instead of commenting on the grades (which Casey was already upset about), I said: "Your teachers seem really pleased with how you cooperate in class. I'm really proud of that. Now we just need to work on the other."

UNCOVERING DISCIPLINE PROBLEMS

N ot all discipline methods follow these principles. Why do some approaches work and others don't? Let's examine a few common discipline methods that don't work.

● *"How could you be so stupid!?"* Abusive language is one technique parents use. It's a form of *coercive* discipline. This method controls a teenager through physical or psychological power. Using name-calling, strong language, yelling and screaming— even slapping—the parent tries to hurt the teenager as much as the disobedience hurt the parent.

Coercive discipline does control a teenager. But it can be self-defeating. According to a Search Institute study published in *The Quicksilver Years*, young people treated in this manner eventually learn to lie or hide their real behavior. They often become adults with poor social skills, low self-esteem and a negative outlook on life.

● *"Sit down and let me tell you a thing or two!"* This milder form of coercive discipline controls through intimidation and badgering. Lecturing is one-way communication with the parent talking. But lecturing isn't teaching.

Teenagers tune out parents in the same way they tune out boring teachers. The brief attention span of younger teenagers guarantees they won't listen to a lengthy lecture. Older teenagers believe they've already heard all parents have to say anyway. They may be quiet, but are they really listening?

● *"Get out of my sight!"* This discipline approach uses *love withdrawal*, manipulating teenagers through parental pouting, silence, expressions of disappointment, avoiding the child, or sulking.

Love withdrawal is easy to use. It doesn't take much time, and parents don't have to deal with teenagers' moods or listen to complaints.

Love withdrawal is dangerous. Experts say adults who were ignored as children learn to hide their true feelings. As they parent, these adults then stifle their own children's emotions. In some cases, emotionally inhibited teenagers turn to using drugs and other dangerous behavior to numb their pain and gain acceptance.

● *"Shape up, or you know what'll happen!"* One of the least-effective discipline methods uses *empty threats*. Threats fall into two main kinds. The first kind are the ones never carried out. For example, a parent threatens to take away the car but never does. The other kind of threats involve unreasonable or illogical consequences. For example, "If you don't clean your room, I'll never buy you another outfit."

Initially, fear of punishment changes a teenager's behavior. But as time passes and a threat never materializes, a teenager realizes the permissive nature of this discipline and grows harder to control with every empty threat.

● *"Whatever you want to do is okay with me!"* This *permissive* style uses casual and accidental discipline. Boundaries aren't strongly defined. Behavior isn't monitored. This parent lacks or has relinquished control.

Teenagers may verbally applaud a permissive parent, but se-

"Yeah I know we have more to talk about. But I better get off the phone in case someone else wants to use it."

cretly resent the neglect. "I don't think my folks love me anymore," Julia sobbed. "They don't even care when I come home." The other kids in the youth group thought Julia had it made—her own car, a big house, every possession she wanted. Later, even they realized Julia's parents were too busy to care.

A teenager with a permissive parent often seeks comfort and security elsewhere, usually in the wrong places. Julia found hers with a college student. She married at 18 and divorced at 20.

● *"You're grounded!"* Restriction means different things to each family. Some parents use it to limit teenagers' activities with friends. Others prevent teenagers from using the telephone, watching television or doing some other activity.

Restriction is often the choice of the *authoritarian* parent. This parent says, "Do it my way or get out!" This parenting style enforces inflexible rules and non-negotiable dictums. When rules are broken, swift punishment follows.

Some Christian parents tend to use this style of discipline, citing Colossians 3:20: "Children, obey your parents in everything, for this pleases the Lord." Young people struggling with self-image easily succumb to a domineering parent. Strong-willed teenagers, however, rebel and deceive their parents.

The problem comes from parents' perception of their role in their teenagers' lives. There's a difference between the *authoritarian* parent and the *authoritative* parent. The authoritarian is a dictator. The authoritative parent is a negotiator. The authoritarian seeks control. The authoritative parent offers guidance, not total control.

Of course, the home is not an absolute democracy. Parents don't yield all authority. Nor should we. Parents still make most final decisions, but the authoritative parent includes the maturing teenager in the discipline process. In addition to Colossians 3:20, authoritative parents remember Colossians 3:21: "Do not embitter your children, or they will become discouraged."

DISCOVERING DISCIPLINE THAT WORKS

*W*e've looked at several discipline methods that tend not to work. Fortunately, creative methods *do* work. They let us keep control while at the same time involving our teenagers in the process. The following examples illustrate creative discipline.

● *"You need to be off the telephone by 10 p.m., or you'll lose the privilege of having the phone in your room."* Sounds like a threat. Looks like a threat. But it's not a threat! It's a statement of fact. This statement sets boundaries and identifies a reasonable consequence.

Our daughter, Casey, talked on the phone well past midnight one Friday night. I was out of town and tried for 90 minutes to let my husband know why I was late. When I returned home, Casey and I talked about the problem. She suggested adding "call waiting" to our phone (and phone bill). I suggested taking the phone out of her room. We settled on a telephone curfew. Realizing that removing her phone was well within my ability, she has been more careful with her telephone calls.

The creative parent says, "I understand your point of view. So what about ..." Proverbs 15:1 cautions, "A gentle answer

turns away wrath, but a harsh word stirs up anger." Instead of an
angry or an uncontrolled reaction, this method seeks balance
through two-way communication.

Creative discipline encourages growth and positive self-
esteem. Teenagers who contribute to discipline decisions feel
better about their abilities and self-worth. Being included in the
process teaches decision-making skills. Your listening and shar-
ing show teenagers how to relate to others. And teenagers develop diplomacy and flexibility as parents and teenagers grapple
with compromise.

Many parents try to use creative methods. Paul endorsed
this style in Ephesians 6:4: "Fathers, do not exasperate your children; instead, bring them up in the training and instruction of
the Lord."

● ***"Where are you going? When will you be back?"*** This
is an inductive method of creative discipline. It took Corey a
while to realize that straight answers to these two questions
satisfied us. Over and over we explained our concern for knowing where he was going and when he'd return. This approach
taught Corey to set his own curfew time.

Inductive discipline allows the teenager a voice in discipline.
While maturing, he or she learns the need to set limits and
develops an awareness of how to function while remaining
aware of others' rights. Both parents and teenagers learn to respect and cultivate positive relationships.

REAPING THE REWARDS OF CREATIVE DISCIPLINE

*R*eplacing the cycle of negative discipline with creative discipline requires concentrated effort. You have to be willing to discard techniques that don't work. Changing old discipline patterns takes time. And occasionally you'll lapse into that old, ineffective behavior. Keep trying—the results are well worth the effort.

Just as there are no perfect teenagers, there are also no perfect parents. And there's no guarantee that new techniques will improve our relationship with our teenagers. What is guaranteed is that guiding teenagers involves taking risks.

One evening the phone jangled me out of my personal time. The voice identified itself as Corey's algebra teacher. "I thought you ought to know that Corey's not turning in his homework. And his last two test grades were very low. He's usually a good student. I hoped maybe you'd know what to do."

I was stunned. "Thank you for calling," I managed before I hung up the phone. I didn't think there was any unusual reason for Corey's doing so poorly. I really believed he was settling for mediocrity.

When Corey came home I confronted him with the teacher's report. Angry words spilled out. How dare I criticize him. It wasn't his fault that he didn't understand math. Before he stormed upstairs I explained that I would help him with his math each night until his grades improved. A slammed door ended the conversation.

I didn't sleep much that night. My stomach stayed knotted. My mind asked unanswerable questions: Would he ever grow up? Was I doing something wrong? Why was I always the villain? I

HOW DO YOU DISCIPLINE?

*E*valuate your own discipline methods by taking this quiz. Select one answer for each question. Use the key on page 17 to total your points and evaluate your discipline style.

1. What discipline method do you use most often with your teenager?
   a. discussing the problem and offering choices
   b. designing the punishment to fit the crime
   c. lecturing or grounding
   d. letting my teenager make personal decisions
   e. threatening

2. How would you classify your discipline style?
   a. open and willing to listen to explanation
   b. consistent and balanced
   c. restrictive and rigid
   d. inconsistent and confusing
   e. permissive and lenient

3. When you were a teenager, how would you have completed this sentence? When I'm a parent I'll ...
   a. encourage my teenager to make his or her own decisions and live with the consequences.
   b. try to be fair and consistent in the way I discipline my teenager.
   c. always trust my teenager.
   d. never punish my teenager the way I was punished.
   e. let my teenager set his or her own curfews with no restrictions.

continued

4. Most of the time, who makes the decision on how to discipline the teenager in your household?
a. my teenager and I
b. my spouse and I jointly decide
c. me
d. my spouse
e. my teenager

5. How effective would you rate your discipline?
a. very effective
b. often effective
c. okay
d. often not effective
e. a failure

6. What would indicate to you that you were a successful disciplinarian?
a. a teenager who keeps communication lines open even after being disciplined
b. a teenager who becomes a well-rounded adult
c. a teenager who always obeys me
d. a teenager who obeys me some of the time
e. a teenager who doesn't rebel

● If you answered mostly d's and e's—You tend to be more lenient than decisive in your discipline. Look for ways to firm up your expectations and boundaries as you continue to read this book.

● If you answered mostly c's—You tend to be authoritarian. Look for ways to broaden your discipline outlook as you continue to read this book.

● If you answered mostly a's and b's—You tend to use authoritative or democratic discipline. Look for additional ideas to enhance your discipline skills as you read this book.

knew I rode Corey's emotional roller coaster along with him.

The next morning I stood at the window waiting for his school bus to appear. Suddenly he stopped behind me, grasping me in a big hug. "I'm sorry, Mom. I shouldn't have blown up last night. You aren't the one who's failing math. I am. Thanks for offering help. I'll fix it. I promise!" And he did.

Another argument. Another sleepless night. Another promise. And yes, another warm, unexpected hug. But the dilemma of how to discipline without damaging relationships and personalities remains.

Effective, creative discipline is a challenge. It's not easy. But the results of discovering a budding, wonderful adult inside that searching, confused teenager make it all worthwhile.

A verse I cling to while guiding both my teenagers through these growing-up years is "Those who sow in tears will reap with songs of joy" (Psalm 126:5).

TIME OUT

1. Make a list of seven words from the following choices that best describe your view of discipline. Ask your teenager to make a separate list of seven words that reflect his or her view of discipline.

Instruction	Explanation
Punishment	Restriction
Training	Practice
Limitation	Judgment
Education	Protection
Retribution	Constraint
Preparation	Edification
Correlation	Regulation

2. Compare your teenager's word choices to your choices. Discuss whether each of you sees discipline as a positive way of guidance or a negative way of punishment.

3. Evaluate your discipline goals. What do you want to achieve through your discipline with your teenager? Discuss these goals with a friend or your spouse. As you read this book, look for specific ways to reach this goal.

CHAPTER **TWO**

❖

DO AWAY WITH DISCIPLINE DEFICIENCIES

❖

How effective are curfews if my teenager constantly misses them?

What's the best time to use isolation?

Why won't my teenager accept no for an answer?

Why doesn't grounding change my teenager's behavior?

These and other questions plague parents of teenagers. Discipline methods that used to work suddenly seem only marginally useful. As teenagers change and develop, parents often don't know how to adjust their discipline methods. Occasionally parents use a discipline method so often that it loses effect. Sometimes parents coping with their own problems can't cope with discipline problems. The next two chapters look at some ways to replace deficient discipline methods with creative strategies that *work*.

How about you? Check your reactions to the following statements to evaluate your own discipline.

	Usually	Often	Some-times	Never
1. I scream when disciplining my teenager.	☐	☐	☐	☐
2. I get angry at my teenager's behavior.	☐	☐	☐	☐
3. I change my mind about how to discipline my teenager.	☐	☐	☐	☐
4. I warn my teenager about wrong behavior even when I have no basis for the warning.	☐	☐	☐	☐
5. I don't know how to respond to my teenager's problem behavior.	☐	☐	☐	☐
6. I punish my teenager more than I want.	☐	☐	☐	☐
7. Life with my teenager is a constant battle.	☐	☐	☐	☐

Total the marks in each column.

● If you answered mostly "sometimes" and "never," congratulations. You've tended to keep these harmful deficiencies out of your discipline.

● If you answered mostly "usually" and "often," you may wonder why discipline doesn't change your teenager's behavior.

Let's look at these and other deeds that rob discipline of its potential for good.

DISCIPLINE DON'TS

*A*t a recent meeting at Casey's school, parents said their #1 fear was losing their teenagers—not only through loss of life, but also through drugs and adversely influential friends.

Fear's a powerful motivator in parenting, isn't it? Parents want to protect their teenagers, but their fears sometime play havoc with rational thinking. In the process of protecting, discipline often sinks to negative punishment. To avoid this, consider practicing the following don'ts.

● **DON'T tell.** As a young child, your son or daughter listened to what you told him or her and obeyed out of fear. Telling deteriorates in efficiency as a teenager's desire for freedom increases. To defend that freedom a teenager will quickly turn your talking into an argument.

Try negotiation.

Telling Corey when to be home worked when he was younger. Almost from the day Corey turned 16, however, we let him set his curfew. Our goal was to encourage him to manage his life and to meet his commitments. Each time he left, he stated when he'd be home. If the time was later than we thought best, we suggested another time. Usually we worked out a compromise time. Corey missed very few curfews when he set them himself.

● **DON'T maintain too many non-negotiable areas.** Non-negotiable areas are unacceptable behaviors that result in strict punishment when broken. One non-negotiable area for me is drug use. Corey watched me work with teenagers on drugs and knew the heart-breaking dangers. This became a non-negotiable area in his friendships too. As a result he came down hard on friends who used drugs, ending a relationship if his friend wouldn't quit.

Most parents maintain a few non-negotiable areas. But too many leave a teenager trapped with no space to learn how to choose.

As a teenager matures, some non-negotiable areas become obsolete. For example, parents may censor revealing clothing choices of a young teenager. As an older teenager settles into acceptable style and dress, the need for firm discipline often disappears.

Occasionally I've examined a non-negotiable area and changed my position. For years school attendance was non-negotiable. My policy was, "You can only miss school if you're running a fever or throwing up. End of discussion."

Circumstances caused me to soften my policy and allow for "mental health" days. Used sparingly, these days provide time to catch up with life after an intense mental, emotional or physical period of pressure.

Casey has taken two mental health days from school since the eighth grade. She recently took a mental health day following her grandmother's funeral. She had several tests at the same time, but couldn't concentrate enough to study. A mental health day allowed her a little extra time to work through the emotionally draining experience.

● **DON'T challenge your teenager with an inappropriate warning.** "If I ever catch you having sex with a guy in this house, you're out of here," warned Alicia's mother.

Her words stunned Alicia who strongly held a Christian conviction that sex outside of marriage was wrong. Besides, she wasn't even dating! Alicia summed up her feelings, "If that's what Mom thinks I'm doing now, I don't stand a chance of doing right in her eyes."

"If ... then ..." accusations defeat discipline. The warning expresses our lack of trust in our teenager. Like any challenge, a warning demands a fight. At the time Alicia didn't know how to reply to her mother. But by the time I talked with her, she wanted to hurt her mother as much as her mother's words had hurt her. Her mom's statement could become a self-fulfilling prophecy. Challenges never work.

● **DON'T use a punishment that's greater than the crime.** And its counterpart, don't compound the error by refusing to admit your mistake. In his ninth grade Corey showed me a low grade on his chemistry test. I came down on him hard.

"Corey, you're capable of doing much better in chemistry. This grade is unacceptable. For the next two weeks I don't want you to watch any television or go out with friends. Come home and work on your chemistry until you get it right." That let him know who was boss!

Corey stomped into his room and slammed the door. About 30 minutes later he returned, and he was angry. "Mom, I didn't have to tell you about that chemistry paper. It's the lowest grade I've gotten in there, but it's not the end of the world. I showed you the paper to let you know how bad my day had been. I didn't think you would crucify me. You've been unfair. Next time I won't show you anything that doesn't have to be signed." And he left again.

Now it was my turn to think. Okay, I'll admit Corey did well in his other subjects. And even after he turned into a "monstrous" teenager, he continued to share good and bad times with me. I decided that the most important issue was not Corey's poor grade, but keeping communication open between us. I went to his room, apologized and removed the restrictions.

Overkill emerges from impulsive anger. This type of anger is an old habit that needs correcting.

A teenager needs to know that lying and damaging property are never acceptable. But no situation calls for abusive anger instead of controlled anger. Abusive anger damages relationships. Harsh punishment, name-calling and impulsive behaviors attack the teenager.

Psychologists believe adults who were emotionally abused as children often use aggressive anger to hide their true feelings. Teenagers respond to abusive anger with fear and loss of respect for a parent. Paul warned in Ephesians 4:26-27 how uncontrolled anger leaves a person open to sin.

It takes conscious effort and practice to control destructive anger. A parent using controlled anger remains calm, even in a maddening situation. This parent speaks quietly but firmly and deals with the issue—not the teenager's character.

● *DON'T use a positive activity as punishment.* Using a positive activity or event to discipline can backfire.

Julie's mom kept her out of youth choir on Sundays when Julie missed her Friday or Saturday night curfew. Then her mom couldn't understand why Julie dropped out of choir.

Adam's dad makes him read a classic novel when he takes away Adam's TV privileges. Adam already resents school. Will home be far behind?

Some parents use scripture memory work as punishment.

These kinds of punishments usually backfire. Teenagers associate these well-intentioned corrections with negative messages. And the positive activity loses its appeal.

TIPS FOR CONTROLLING ANGER

When you recognize you're getting angry, try the following ideas:

1. Call it anger. Say, "I'm getting angry" or "This discussion is making me angry." Warn the other person how you feel.

2. Figure out what causes your anger. You're most susceptible to anger when you're tired, ill or worried.

Be specific as you identify what makes you angry. Don't say, "It's his weird friends." Figure out what about his friends makes you angry. Ecclesiastes 7:8-9 wisely instructs us to refrain from being easily provoked to anger.

3. Look for a way to cool it. "Take note of this. Everyone should be quick to listen, slow to speak and slow to become angry," urges James 1:19. Do what it takes to back off mentally or physically from an explosive situation. Count to 10. Hide in the bathroom for five minutes. Tell your teenager you'll talk when you're not so angry.

4. Study how others handle anger. You act and react as you see it modeled. Choose positive models who control anger (Proverbs 22:24-25).

5. Don't keep it bottled up. Share your anger with someone, even if you can't share it with the person making you angry. Unresolved anger leaves you open to other damaging emotions (Ephesians 4:26-27).

6. Pray. Pray for the person and the situation that make you angry.

● *DON'T attack the teenager or the teenager's friends.*
Name-calling, sarcasm and putdowns destroy fragile teen egos.
Teenagers tend to believe what they hear. Therefore, it's critical
that parents attack the problem—not the teenager.

Mary's daughter Maggie and two friends decided to spend
the night at Jami's house. Around midnight Jami's mother called
to ask if Mary had heard from the girls. "It's past the time when
they said they'd be in. I'm concerned." Mary woke up her husband, Bob, and together they waited. Around 1 a.m., with no
word from the girls, all of the parents gathered at Jami's house.
Apprehension mounted until the girls came in around 2:30 a.m.

Without waiting for explanations, Mary and Bob immediately escorted Maggie home. On the way, Bob took charge. "Can
you explain why you were more than three hours later than the
time you said you'd be at Jami's?" Mary was so mad she can't remember Maggie's few lame excuses.

Bob continued, "While we're glad you're safe, several fam-
ilies have been disrupted because the four of you decided to
cruise around and miss your curfew. In the past, we trusted you
to keep your word. Tonight you didn't. We'll talk about the consequences tomorrow."

The next day Mary and Bob asked Maggie to write notes of
apology to each girl's parents. She also apologized in person to
Jami's mother. And she couldn't spend evenings out for a
month. In addition, the other parents agreed to talk to their
daughters about decision-making skills.

When Mary told me the story she exclaimed, "I was so angry, embarrassed and hurt by Maggie's thoughtlessness, I
couldn't think of anything nice to say to her. She should be glad
her dad handled the situation, instead of me. I would've used
words intended to hurt her."

"Hi, these are the peers to whom I relate in order to break away from you and become a fully functioning, self-reliant adult."

In addition to not attacking your teenager, refrain from attacking his or her friends. Teenagers personalize negative statements against their friends. When you remain pleasant to these friends, your teenager can't use your attack as an excuse to rebel.

This "don't" has an exception. If you're concerned for your teenager's life or health, act quickly.

Unfortunately, forbidding a teenager to see a friend is difficult to control. When Bill realized his son's friends were drug dealers, he refused to let them near his house. Bill also sought professional counseling and, eventually, drug rehabilitation for his son.

My top fear for teenagers involves their latching on to the wrong crowd. A few rebellious friends can quickly lead a teenager astray. Be wary. Remain cautious. Spend time talking with your teenager's friends. Find out what's happening in their lives. But through it all, don't attack your teenager. And be polite to your teenager's friends.

● *Don't use lengthy solitary confinement.* Isolation gives both you and your teenager time apart to cool down before confronting a problem. But extended time alone as a punishment usually doesn't change behavior.

Teenagers like being alone, especially in this electronic age in which a set of headphones connected to a radio, television or cassette player tunes out the world. Time alone prevents them from learning how to grow socially adept with family and peers.

When I isolated Corey, I gave him something to do such as, "Figure out how you can bring up your grades." At the end of isolation he'd share his thoughts.

● *Don't use empty threats.* When asked what they'd do

differently to discipline their kids, many parents reply: "I wish I could take back all those empty threats. They wasted my energy and insulted my teenager's intelligence." Empty threats also weaken a parent's authority.

Cecil's warning to take away Corey's car was basically ineffective. Cecil used this threat often but carried it out only once. I told Cecil that taking away Corey's car punished me, because I had to chauffeur him around. A more effective discipline—and one we used—restricted Corey's car use to specific times, such as driving to and from school or to work.

THE PARENT'S VIEWPOINT

*M*ost parents want a peaceful home. Daily discipline decisions, however, can't be avoided. And that daily discipline may not be peaceful. There are several reasons that discipline is more unpleasant for some parents than for others.

● *Power vs. authority*—Some parents confuse power with authority. Superior force backs power. Insight and fairness strengthen authority.

Power relies on surrender. Authority relies on respect.

Power bullies, dredges up past mistakes and settles for the easiest way out. Authority remains firm in a tactful, diplomatic way.

Authority recognizes a teenager's self-pity, but refuses to succumb to that pity. Authority doesn't resort to a teenager's childish level with name-calling or uncontrolled anger.

● *Unhappy parents*—Parents who are unhappy with themselves dole out ineffective discipline. Tom's dad often punishes Tom for a trait he sees in his own life. "I'm quick to recognize Tom's aggressive temper. I punish him whenever he uses it—probably because I don't like my own temper."

Jay has another kind of problem with his mom. "Why is she always screaming and crying? Why does she get so angry over nothing?" Jay reaped the stress of the biological changes happening to his mother in menopause. When Jay's mother went through menopause, she was unhappy with her changing body. Unintentionally she sometimes took out her frustration on Jay. Why God put mothers with raging hormones and teenagers with fluctuating hormones in the same house is one of those questions I plan to ask God someday.

● *Scapegoats*—A parent who assumes total responsibility for a teenager's actions and feelings makes poor discipline decisions. Parental guilt over a teenager's mistakes can result in a sense of failure and helplessness for the parent. As developing adults, teenagers share the responsibility of growing up.

Occasionally a parent refuses to recognize the real problem. That parent may blame a teenager's actions on diet or an illness. A teenager with diabetes bragged about her ability to get away with anything, because her parents felt sorry for her. This inability to recognize the causes of a teenager's misbehavior keeps discipline ineffective.

● *Divided parents*—In two-parent homes—and also in single-parent homes—teenagers often pit one parent against another. If a teenager doesn't receive the desired reply from one parent, he or she may go to the other parent with the same request. If parents fail to communicate, teenagers quickly learn how to divide and conquer. The result is a lack of discipline. Parents who fail to define discipline boundaries or who make false assumptions shouldn't be surprised by the lack of control over teenagers.

● *Kids don't listen.* Parents complain that discipline doesn't work because teenagers don't listen. Kids have an immense capacity to tune out the world around them—especially teachers and parents. The next chapter suggests ways to increase communication so a teenager does listen.

THE TEENAGER'S VIEWPOINT

*L*ike parents, teenagers notice ineffective discipline. They have their own reasons why discipline doesn't always work.

● *No reason for discipline*—Teenagers are frustrated by discipline administered without sufficient reason. "Just because I'm the parent" sounds valid to a parent, but is inadequate to a teenager. Giving reasons may not always be possible, but teenagers tend to cooperate if they know why.

The first New Year's Eve after Corey got his driver's license he wanted to stay out late. A firm no only resulted in complaints. Cecil finally explained our concern about the increased number of drunk drivers on the road. Corey still fussed but knew our position was right. He came in by 12:30 a.m.

● *Inconsistency*—Parental inconsistency ranks high on a teenager's list of discipline complaints. Inconsistency creates confusion for the teenager who never knows how a parent will react to similar offenses.

Teenagers quickly point out inconsistent treatment parents give to brothers and sisters. "Mom always liked you best!" whines Dick Smothers to his brother Tom. We laugh at the classic Smothers Brothers' comedy routine because of its familiarity. Parents recognize, however, that children have unique personalities requiring varied discipline. Siblings don't see the differences.

● *Forced promises*—Teenagers deeply resent any discipline that requires them to make promises they know they won't keep. Jerry told me: "Karen won't get involved with drugs. I made her promise never to touch them." As a seventh-grader, Karen should be able to keep that promise. But what about when she's in the 11th grade?

Many parents ask their teenagers to sign a "no drinking and driving" covenant. This covenant provides an appropriate standard of commitment for 16-year-olds who face the issue every time they leave the house. To a 13-year-old who can't drive, the document is meaningless.

● *Stress*—Parental stress is a final area teenagers believe creates ineffective discipline. Sometimes a parent brings anger home after a rough day at work and takes it out on the teenager. Other times it's parental pressure on kids to excel in school, to win on the sports field, to live up to an older sibling's reputation or to fulfill a parent's dream. This parental pressure grows from the parent's need, not the teenager's.

Rob dreams about a future of operating a country store in a

rural community, not filling the high-powered position his dad sees for him in the Fortune 500. Rob makes the grades to please his dad. But secretly, he'd like to live a calmer, less-pressured life.

● ● ●

You're probably thinking "I don't stand a chance. I do all the wrong things." While some discipline methods don't work, there are several discipline techniques that are effective. You might even be using one or two and don't realize it.

Don't give up. Remember, you weren't born knowing how to raise a teenager. The fact that you're still reading this book shows you really care about helping your teenager develop. Eliminating the negatives is part of the process. Replacing them with effective discipline completes the process. That's the focus of the rest of the book.

TIME OUT

1. Describe your vision of your relationship with your teenager by the time that teenager finishes high school. What will you have to change to make it happen?

2. Look through "The Teenager's Viewpoint" on discipline on page 32. Which one or two problems do you find yourself falling prey to more often? In the next week, work to overcome the negative discipline that results from each problem.

CHAPTER*THREE*

❖

DEVELOP THE DISCIPLINE ADVANTAGE

❖

C *ase Study #1:* You've experienced no major problems with your 11th-grade teenager until now. You think your teenager is drinking, but you're not sure. What would you do?

Case Study #2: Your high school senior chronically over-spends her paycheck. She's always borrowing money from you or friends. She promises to pay you back but rarely does. What would you do?

Case Study #3: On your family vacation your 16-year-old son tells you he's been smoking for several months. What would you do?

There are no pat answers to these situations. Each response

depends on the teenager's personality, the parent's level of trust and the history of that relationship. In this chapter we'll look at suggestions for working through these and other discipline problems. There are no magic formulas, just a few ideas to broaden our approach to discipline.

DISCIPLINE DO'S

*T*he most beneficial discipline methods change teenagers' inappropriate behavior or help them learn from the experience. Let these "do's" start us thinking about some ways to move toward creative discipline.

● *DO teach, instead of preach.* In ninth grade Casey brought home a poor score on her biology test. Needing a parent's signature, she brought the test paper to me with a full explanation. "Mom, I'm really sorry I didn't do well on this test. I can do better next time. I didn't leave enough time to study. It won't happen again. If you think I need to quit watching television for a week I will."

I began, "Casey, I'm disappointed in this grade. And you're right, you can do better. When is your next test?" I'd learned my lesson about overkill with Corey. Instead of restricting her activities, I wanted to help her deal with the problem of poor preparation.

"Next Friday," she replied hesitantly.

"Then, Thursday night I'll help you study for your test."

Casey grumbled, but on Thursday night she brought me her

biology textbook. Together we reviewed the chapter. I drilled her repeatedly on the terms and charts until I felt she understood the material. The next day she easily aced the test. The discipline centered on improving her study skills. Along the way, she learned the material. In fact, several times during that year she asked for help in studying biology.

No amount of preaching would've increased her study skills nor improved her willingness to learn. Instead of talking, I showed her.

● *DO allow time to process a problem.* Rather than punish impulsively, back away either physically or emotionally to think through the problem. Let's apply this technique to the case of the drinking teenager (Case Study #1).

Be sure there's a problem. Without strong evidence, confrontation is the least-effective approach. Accusations without a foundation result in denial and distrust. Bring up the suspected problem—in this case drinking—at a time other than during a crisis. For example, if you and your teenager hear a newscast on teenage drinking, ask your teenager questions similar to these: Do a lot of kids at your school drink? How do you feel about drinking? Why do kids your age drink?

Change your own pattern of behavior, if necessary, to identify the problem. If you normally go to bed, wait up for your teenager to come home. This surprise greeting can tell you a lot.

Once you discover your teenager is drinking or using drugs, act immediately. Some teenagers respond to grounding or restriction. Consider other options too. One mother took her son to several Alcoholics Anonymous meetings for teenagers. Another family looked under "Alcohol and Drugs" in the Yellow Pages and found a local agency that offered help. In addition to sending useful literature, the agency provided a free evaluation of the teenager's problem. One family rented a videotape showing how alcohol impairs a driver's skills. The parents watched the video with the teenager, then used it to discuss their boundaries on drinking.

● *DO network with other parents who share similar beliefs and values.* Why don't parents stay in touch with one another more often? Usually it's a matter of not taking the time to compare notes. Or a parent may be embarrassed by appearing unable to manage a teenager. Parents frequently don't realize that others experience similar trials.

Parent workshops and support groups sponsored by your church, school or community provide an opportunity to share discipline and ideas that work and those that don't. These groups may also offer potential solutions to problems. And consider talking with your church's youth minister.

Exposure to other teenagers also helps. After their dad taught ninth-grade Sunday school for six months, Austin's two teenagers thanked me for recruiting him. "Dad's not so hard on us anymore."

Austin later laughed. "Once I saw what other kids were like," he explained, "I realized mine weren't all that abnormal."

● *DO set reasonable limits.* Reasonable boundaries teach your teenager self-discipline. Instead of restricting, they allow a teenager to make choices. Let's apply setting reasonable limits to the case of the girl who has trouble with money (Case Study #2).

We faced a similar situation with Corey. Money slid through his fingers. We tried several discipline approaches—doling out half his paycheck each week, letting him pay back a loan in

"Well, see it's like this, Steve and I were on our way home when a flour truck ran us off the road into a ditch, then a pack of wild dogs in the field attacked us, so we had to go to the emergency room to be treated for rabies, but a pregnant woman was rushed in so we were told to wait . . . "

small doses and refusing to loan him any money.

Combined with other problems, Corey realized his need for professional help. Corey set the appointment and went on his own. At that first meeting, the psychiatrist related a principle that changed Corey's life. "Some people are controlled by their circumstances. Others control their circumstances. You're in the first group. During these sessions our goal will be to move you into the second group."

The process involved Corey's setting limits on specific areas of his life. Corey told us—and later so did the professional—that we contributed to Corey's being controlled by his circumstances by unintentionally supporting his borrowing habit. We, therefore, refused to supplement Corey's adequate summer income. These and other limitations gave Corey a chance to regain control in his life. Last summer he worked, went to school and paid his expenses without our help.

● *DO maintain a sense of humor.* "Loosen up, Mom," Corey advised me once. He was right. I didn't use humor nearly enough with him. When appropriate, humor can lighten the tension. The danger, of course, is using humor *against* your teenager in ways that put him or her down.

● *DO appeal to a teenager's self-worth.* Day-to-day affirmation of your teenager greatly enhances discipline. Praise motivates behavior more strongly than criticism. Daily hugs and smiles reassure your teenager of your support. Let's apply this idea to the case of the smoking teenager (Case Study #3).

Once again, this case study actually happened. After two weeks of a three-week summer vacation, Corey was helping me do a load of laundry.

"Mom, I guess you're wondering why I've been so hard to live with on this trip," he began. (I thought he was just another teenager experiencing too much family togetherness.) "I'm sorry to tell you this, but I've been smoking for a while. I guess I'm addicted, because I've sure been nervous." His downcast eyes underscored the pain of that confession. He couldn't believe that bumming cigarettes off friends had left him addicted.

My heart hurt. Cecil smokes. As a child Corey adamantly tried to get his dad to quit. I never dreamed Corey would start smoking.

"I remember how hard it was to quit smoking," I told Corey. "I smoked some in college and afterward. But I hated my smelly clothes and dirty ashtrays, so I quit. It took a long time to get over that desire for a cigarette."

"How did you quit?" he asked curiously.

"I stopped cold. But it wasn't easy. What can I do to help you quit smoking?" I asked, not sure where the conversation was going. We talked about several options. Then I stated a few guidelines. "Please don't smoke in my presence or in Casey's. Please smoke only in the den with the fan on or go outside. You'll be responsible for cleaning up your ashtrays. If they're not kept clean, I'll throw them away."

As we got ready to leave the laundry I pulled Corey close and told him how much I loved him, how important his health was to me and how sorry I was that he was going through this struggle. I told him I'd do anything to help him stop any time.

Several months later Corey disclosed the significance of that conversation. "I dreaded telling you, because I thought you'd be so angry. I was surprised by what you said and did. That's when I knew you really cared about *me* and not the way I acted."

Thank you, Lord, for helping me say something right.

● *DO listen without judging.* Focus on the problem not the teenager. One weekend Cecil and I went out of town, leaving Corey at home with a friend. When we returned Corey blurted out the events of Saturday night. He and his buddy planned to "TP" another friend's house. Before they could toss the first toilet paper roll, they saw a police car approaching in the distance. They quickly hid under a parked car. After the police car glided by, they abandoned their plan and hurried home.

Their close encounter with the law frightened Corey. While telling me the story he realized, "You trusted me to behave while you were gone, and I didn't. I promise it won't happen again."

How should I have responded? blow up? ground him for a month? No, I just listened. Telling me the story was punishment enough, knowing how I feel about damaging another's property.

Later, we focused on the real problem of Corey's breaking our trust. We talked about trust and its importance in a relationship. It took another trip out of town to show him the need for trust.

The next time Cecil and I left town, grandmother stayed with the kids. Because she was extremely finicky, the kids eagerly anticipated our return. After that we left Corey alone at home during other weekend trips and never had another problem.

● *DO act with redemption.* The parables of Jesus and his encounters with others reveal the richness of his redemption. In Luke 15 the prodigal son returned to the open arms and forgiving spirit of his father. Jesus didn't condemn the adulterous woman in John 8:3-11. Instead, he forgave her and challenged her to live righteously. Forgiveness, like love, must be given again and again.

DISCIPLINE STEPS

Wouldn't it be wonderful if teenagers acted as predicted in all these books about living with teenagers? You'd have the perfect answer for each situation.

Corey hadn't been a teenager very long before he realized, "Mom, for someone who's supposed to understand teenagers, you sure don't!" He was absolutely right. After working with teenagers for more than 20 years, theory clashed with reality when it came to disciplining Corey. Even when Corey acted like a normal teenager, I wondered if our family would survive his adolescence. You've probably had similar thoughts.

The following steps might help you pull these discipline do's and don'ts together. Begin with a willingness to think and act deliberately. Don't become discouraged too quickly. If you'll hang in there, you'll discover that your discipline will be more creative and effective.

Step 1: Eliminate the negatives. By now, you've identified actions and attitudes limiting creative discipline. Removing negatives means you'll respond to your teenager's rudeness with politeness. It means you'll speak calmly when confronted by an angry teenager. It also means you won't give up if you blow it. Undoing negative habits takes persistence.

Think before acting. Ask yourself how a different response could affirm your teenager while dealing with the problem.

Above all, pray about your relationship and attitude toward your teenager. God answers prayers for wisdom, understanding and reconciliation in unique and wonderful ways.

Step 2: Replace negatives with positives. Alcoholics

Anonymous warns family members to replace old patterns of relating to the alcoholic with new behavior. A family no longer needs to nag or fight or care for the alcoholic. Family members rebuild relationships on new interests and shared activities once abandoned but now restored.

Do the same with your teenager. Build a different relationship as you eliminate those negatives of nagging and telling. Discover common interests. Become involved in the world of your teenager. Attend school events. Chaperone church activities—with your teenager's permission—of course.

Step 3: Remember that discipline is affirmation as well as correction. Many examples in this book deal with problems. But discipline is much more than punishment. Creative discipline reinforces positive behavior. A sincere compliment, an appropriate thank-you, a smile, a hug or a pat on the back assures your teenager: "You're special to me. I'm proud of you!"

My personal goal each day includes stroking any positive behavior. It might be as simple as thanking Casey for going with me to the grocery store on the way home from school. (Not her favorite activity, but at least she didn't gripe.)

Step 4: Disarm the difficult. Disarm the complaining teenager by agreeing when possible. I learned this trick from my mother. She'd say, "I agree that it seems unfair. Can you think of another solution?" Agreeing with the complainer takes the wind out of a complaint.

Disarm the challenger by answering the teenager's question with a question. Jesus did this repeatedly with the scribes and Pharisees who challenged his every move. Probably the most memorable is his response to their question about his authority

(Matthew 21:23-27). Responding with a question buys time and allows your teenager to see your side of an issue.

Disarm teenagers by seeing a situation from their viewpoint. Your teenagers will appreciate your willingness to focus on their feelings. Cecil called from the emergency room early one morning to say Corey had been in an automobile accident. He had a slight memory loss after a bad bump on the head.

When Corey came home I wanted to lecture him on the need to wear a seat belt. (He wouldn't have hit his head.) I wanted to remind him to ride with careful drivers. I didn't. The time was inappropriate. Instead, I concentrated on helping him deal with the emotional trauma of the accident.

● ● ●

Put these do's into action as quickly as possible to erase the don'ts. Not all ideas work every time. Experiment until you find the right combination. Perhaps your teenager will notice your efforts and even cooperate.

TIME OUT

1. List specific traits, abilities and attitudes you like about your teenager. During the next week praise your teenager for these traits. Or write a note of appreciation stating these qualities. Keep your list for a time when the negatives threaten your relationship.

2. Which discipline "do" would be the most difficult for you to achieve? Talk with a friend or your spouse about it. Test the idea to see how it works.

3. Ask your teenager to respond to a case study at the beginning of this chapter as if he or she were the parent. Your teenager's comments will give you insight into a teenager's way of thinking.

CHAPTER **FOUR**

❖

DON'T MAJOR ON THE MINORS

❖

**P**ick your battles carefully," an experienced friend advised. Cecil and I soon learned the value of her advice. Every area of life can turn into a battlefield between parents and teenagers. But is it necessary to fight over every issue? Are some more important than others?

Listed below are several potential conflicts common to teenagers. Circle those that are of major importance to you as you discipline your teenager.

bedroom	movies
clothing	concerts
hair/makeup	amount of spending money
language	use of spending money
sex	dating
choice of friends	curfew

where teenager goes	bedtime
time of return	eating habits
drug use	drinking
quality of school work	personal hygiene
music	church attendance
bathroom condition after use	manners

Depending on the day's events and your current level of frustration, you may have circled almost every item. On another day when tensions ease, you might circle only a few.

This morning I would circle "bathroom condition after use." Casey's bathroom would normally withstand a lenient inspection. But this morning, it's different. A friend stayed with Casey over the weekend. On this Monday morning, wet towels hang from every rack, and the hamper overflows with sheets, sweaters, pants and other assorted clothing.

After looking at this bathroom, I want to ask Casey why she couldn't carry those wet towels to the laundry room. I want her to explain why she continued to jam clothing into the overflowing hamper. I want to, but I won't. By the time she arrives home this afternoon, the towels will be fluffed and back on the shelf, the laundry will be clean, and Casey will eagerly tell me about her day. I could bring up the bathroom issue, but it would shorten the pleasant time we'll spend together.

Why won't I make "bathroom condition after use" an issue with Casey? There are several reasons. Most of the time, she leaves the bathroom in pretty good shape. By placing her dirty clothes in the hamper and hanging all the towels on the racks, she obeyed the basic family rule. I also want her to keep inviting her friends into our home.

There's one more reason why "bathroom condition after use" won't escalate into a major problem. Several weeks ago

Casey and her friend Sarah raced in from school, diligently completed their homework, woofed down dinner, quickly did hair and makeup, and hurried to a Bible study at church.

The bathroom was a mess. Makeup spread over the counter. Hair dryers hung from unusual places. Towels hid in one corner, discarded clothes in another.

Wow, I was mad! I stepped through the mess and closed the door.

During her absence, I mentally reviewed the key points I wanted to cover. I prepared and polished my speech. I was ready to let her have it when Casey skipped through the back door around 9:30 p.m. Before I could say a word, she began, "Gosh, Mom, I'm sorry we left the bathroom in such a mess. We just had so little time. I hope it didn't upset you too much. Let me clean it up, then I'll tell you what happened tonight at Bible study." She darted upstairs before I could say a word.

I spoke aloud into the empty space, "And don't you forget it."

While picking up the bathroom, "condition of bathroom after use" was major. By that afternoon, it shrunk back to its usual minor status.

ABOUT THE MAJORS

*E*arly in my role as mother, I discovered several areas worth worrying about, while others didn't matter. By the time our children were teenagers, and all of us in the throes of change, Cecil and I needed to focus on a few discipline issues that mattered most to us. Certain criteria defined these majors.

• *The health and safety of our teenagers*—Two questions—"Where are you going?" and "What time will you return?"—give us important information that help determine whether activities are safe and healthy. If we discover our teenagers didn't go where they said they were going or if they return home later than anticipated, discipline follows. Of course, a telephone call and a reasonable explanation keep us informed of changing plans.

Kevin's sudden withdrawal from the family at first appeared to be minor "teenageritis." Soon, however, Jim and Jean made his withdrawal a major issue.

To deal with the problem, they invited Kevin to join them for a day at a nearby amusement park. At first Kevin hesitated. But when they insisted, he agreed.

"I thought Kevin would pout all day," Jean recalled. "Instead everyone had a great time—laughing, competing at the arcade, seeing who could eat the most. It was a wonderful day. And Kevin was the Kevin we knew.

"On the way home, Jim told Kevin about our concern for him. Then, he asked Kevin if we'd done something to make him unhappy."

Jean's smile told the story. "It was like a dam had burst. Kevin had tried marijuana with a couple of kids from school. He didn't like it, but was caught in a cycle of deceit. He felt awful. He didn't know how to tell us."

Jean spoke more confidently now, "We asked Kevin what he wanted us to do. 'Just tell me I can't see those guys anymore,' he replied after a little thought.

"So that's what we did. He told those guys his parents were cracking down on his friends, and he couldn't meet them anymore after school."

IS IT MAJOR OR MINOR?

C hoose an issue from the list at the beginning of the chapter that you judge important. Use the following to test whether the issue is worthy of being a major or should be reduced to a minor.

1. Is the health of the teenager affected by this issue?

     yes ☐   no ☐

2. Can anyone else be harmed by the teenager's behavior in this issue?

     yes ☐   no ☐

3. Is the teenager's best interest served by making this a major?

     yes ☐   no ☐

4. Will discipline correct behavior if this becomes a major?

     yes ☐   no ☐

5. Check the emotions you feel when you think about this issue:

☐ extreme worry   ☐ mild concern
☐ fear   ☐ embarrassment
☐ pain   ☐ anger
☐ hopelessness   ☐ frustration

6. What would be the worst possible result of your teenager's making this issue a problem? Rate the reality of that happening on this graph:

won't happen 1 2 3 4 5 6 7 8 9 10 will happen

If you answered yes to questions 1 to 4, and selected emotions on the left side of question 5, and rated the reality of problem over 6 in question 6, then this is a major problem and deserves your attention.

Their concern for Kevin's health led Jim and Jean to take four creative discipline steps:

1. They included him in a special time with the family.
2. They stated their concern in a relaxed atmosphere.
3. They listened to the problem without growing alarmed.
4. They worked on a solution.

● *Our teenagers' involvement in Christian influences*—Knowing the negative influence of the world on our children's lives, both Cecil and I want to expose our children to positive Christian influences. Majors for us are Sunday school and church attendance. As young teenagers, both of our kids knew church attendance was not optional.

When Corey began driving, however, he challenged our position. If he went out on Saturday night, we expected him to get up for church on Sunday. Of course, he didn't have to go out Saturday night, which made getting up easy.

● *The effect of an act on others*—"Condition of bathroom after use" is not an ongoing problem with Casey. With Corey it was. Both teenagers shared a bathroom, which was also used by family members—as well as guests. Corey often left clothes behind the door, towels on the floor, dripping water in the tub and paraphernalia littering the sink. His careless clutter frustrated the rest of us.

Lectures on courteous behavior didn't work. Threats of limited bathroom privileges also failed. The discipline that worked most often was transferring Corey's mess to his room—wet towels, clean and dirty clothes, hair dryer, everything. Eventually he couldn't find clean clothes, the wet towels smelled, and he got tired of walking around the growing piles in his room. Since

Corey's been at college and lived with people who're even more messy than he, he's discovered the importance of respecting others' space.

Identifying majors and reducing other issues to minors takes deliberate thought and action. Some issues fit easily into one category or the other. Other issues move between being minors and majors.

ABOUT THE MINORS

*M*ost wise parents would agree that it's wise to pick "battles" carefully. Be prepared to defend majors and let minors go. The key to all of this is to use creative discipline with patience and let teenagers work out solutions on their own with positive parental guidance.

Here are a few issues that were minors for us—most of the time!

● *A teenager's room*—Privacy is critical to young people who're sorting out thoughts, attitudes, ideas and values. Personal notebooks and letters are off-limits to parents. Many parents, however, feel responsible for a teenager's room and try to keep these private domains clean.

As small children, Corey and Casey regularly made their beds and straightened their rooms. As teenagers, a clean room was a low priority to them. Rather than nag them about cleaning their rooms, I used a different tactic. I closed the door. I surrendered room responsibilities to them with a sense of real relief.

Two simple rules applied:

1. Dirty clothes must be in the clothes hamper in order to be laundered.

2. It's their job to dust and vacuum their rooms and change their bed linens.

Corey used his hair dryer to dust his shelves. Casey sometimes vacuums her room at midnight. But their rooms aren't my concern. If the disorder grows too chaotic, I close the door.

Some parents feel uncomfortable leaving a teenager's room and personal belongings completely alone. Unless you have a valid reason to distrust your teenager, assume the best, not the worst. Of course, if a teenager is abusing this privacy to hide pornography, take drugs or participate in other dangerous or unhealthy activities, the room becomes a major concern.

● *A teenager's clothing*—This is another area where parental control diminishes as a teenager's ability develops. Once I suggested keeping clothes a minor at a parents' meeting and drew an intriguing response. "I'm afraid of what my friends will say about how Brad dresses." How sad that a mother's worry about her standing with her friends kept her from teaching her teenager skills that would help him function in life.

Even when you disagree with the style or color of your teenager's clothing, remember that clothes help them try on different personalities as they discover who they are. Corey liked secondhand clothes. At least it was fairly inexpensive to clothe him. Even though black didn't flatter his fair coloring, that's what he wore most often.

Although clothing can be a minor, we parents should still offer guidance. Set limits on appropriate clothing. Suggestive or sexually explicit clothing is unacceptable. We need to state our limits clearly. Appropriate apparel for the occasion is another area needing guidance. Corey wasn't allowed to wear shorts to church. If he tried, we sent him home to change.

● *Hair and makeup*—Two other areas to leave in the minor category are hair and makeup. I was a teenager during the '60s when the length of a guy's hair caused parental agony. I vowed hair would not be a battlefield with my children.

I've often wondered why Corey's hair hasn't fallen out with all he did to it. But experimenting with hair colors and styles was his way of discovering who he was. When he asked for my reaction, I tried to be kind.

One day I woke up from a late afternoon nap. Casey informed me Corey had used purple mousse on his hair and gone out. When he came home, I continued fixing dinner without commenting on his hair. Finally, he couldn't stand it any longer. "How do you like my hair, Mom? Don't worry. It'll wash out."

"It's not my favorite thing you've done to your hair. I'm just surprised you went out in public like that."

"Oh, I didn't go out in public. I just went to the mall!"

That's an example of one of those wonderful, illogical teenager remarks. And the story is a favorite, because Corey's hair remained purple for several weeks. His porous hair soaked up the purple mousse, so it didn't wash out quickly.

Corey never used purple mousse again.

In addition to hair, makeup is the girl's side of this issue. Most girls try different colors, intensities and types of makeup to represent the person they are.

If your teenage daughter wants to wear makeup, but you feel she's too young, compromise. Perhaps a soft blusher for the cheeks or a lip gloss would satisfy her. If she really wants heavier makeup, ask a consultant at the beauty counter of a department store to show her how to apply makeup properly. Then have your daughter purchase her own makeup. Young girls usually discover makeup is more trouble than it's worth.

For Casey's 13th birthday, I invited a makeup specialist to attend the party and show the girls how to apply makeup. She gave the girls several helpful ideas. This prevented makeup from becoming a major issue later.

● *Money*—Depending on the way you and your teenager approach the use of money, it will move back and forth between being a major or minor issue.

When Corey first started to ask to go to rock concerts, I responded with an authoritarian no. Later, I told him he had to buy his own tickets. Since concert tickets were so expensive, he rarely saved enough money to go.

In his ninth grade year we set up a checking account for Corey. He quickly learned how to use the automatic teller card. He also learned about being overdrawn, paying for ATM usages and check-writing charges. At different times his spending money became a major. Other times it was a minor.

FROM MINORS TO MAJORS

A few majors start out as harmless minors. Then parents start to worry. "Maybe he needs more sleep. He looks so tired." "I've heard that kids on drugs dress in weird clothing. Is that

WOULD YOU ...?

*M*ost majors and minors develop out of everyday issues. Occasionally an area may need to be major. But usually these daily issues remain minor.

Think about majors and minors in your family. Then take the following "test" to check your reactions in these particular situations. Select only one response for each situation.

1. Your teenage son brings home a friend who's wearing a black leather jacket and an earring. Would you ...
a. go to your bedroom and cry in panic?
b. welcome the young man into your home?
c. warn your teenager about hanging around with people like that?

2. Your daughter bought the latest compact disc with the money you gave her to buy a blouse she needed. Would you ...
a. give her more money for the blouse?
b. let her figure out what to do?
c. make her return the compact disc?

continued

3. You want your son to receive a college scholarship. In his senior year he brings home a C in calculus. Would you . . .

    a. ground him?

    b. praise him for understanding the subject well enough to get a C?

    c. get a tutor to help him bring up his grade?

4. After school your teenager eats a pizza and half a carton of ice cream. Two hours later, she's not hungry for dinner. Would you . . .

    a. send her to her room for the rest of the evening?

    b. ask her to sit at the table while the family eats?

    c. make her eat again?

5. You can't hear your television over your son's stereo. Would you . . .

    a. yell at him to turn it down?

    b. turn up your television?

    c. take the stereo away from him?

If you selected mostly a's or c's, you might be making the situation a major. If you selected mostly b's, the situation is probably a minor. If you selected a's or c's for three or more situations, then perhaps you're majoring on minors.

why she wears that silly hat?" "He's not eating enough." "She's eating too much."

● **Know the difference between healthy worry and useless worry.** Healthy worry keeps parents aware of a teenager's world. It watches and listens but doesn't panic. Healthy worry shows concern—not fear.

Useless worry occurs when parents assume the worst about their teenagers. It drains parents physically as they worry about activities or attitudes beyond their control. Useless worry results in punishment that brings resentment from a teenager.

Jesus addressed useless worry in his Sermon on the Mount. "Therefore do not worry about tomorrow, for tomorrow will worry about itself. Each day has enough trouble of its own," he said in Matthew 6:34. He knew worrying can't change reality. He encouraged his followers to work out the problems for the present and not speculate about what might be.

One night after Corey went to bed I found two large safety pins and a bottle of denatured alcohol on the bathroom counter. All night I tossed and turned, fearing Corey would pierce his ear with a safety pin. The next morning I asked him about the safety pins and alcohol. He explained how he used the alcohol to clean the cut he made while shaving his sideburns. He used the safety pins to hold up the jeans he'd worn the previous day. They were missing a button I hadn't replaced. Oops!

● **Resist the instinct to nag.** Minors become majors when day-to-day frustrations turn into nagging. The heavy beat of a teenager's stereo vibrates just a little too loudly on a stressful day. A slamming door expresses unresolved anger. A teenager's 40-minute shower leaves us taking a tepid bath once again.

"Whattaya mean, it's too loud? I already turned it down once!"

Corey used to take looooooong showers, leaving no hot water for anyone else. We fussed and nagged and threatened. Finally, Cecil, Corey and I agreed that Corey would limit his showers to 20 minutes.

Unfortunately, that idea didn't work, since Corey didn't have a clock in the shower. The next suggestion—and the one that worked most often—was for whoever was waiting for a shower to blink the bathroom light after 15 minutes. Corey knew he had only a few minutes to get out before that person would come in and turn off the water. Locking the bathroom door didn't stop us; we just turned off the circuit breaker. Without a window, that bathroom was awfully dark!

● *Try to stay calm.* Some minors pounce on you without warning. I consider my ability to stay calm a strength. But occasionally I blow it!

Hair was not a big issue with me. It was a little more important to Cecil, who still sports a crew cut. Corey, who has naturally curly, brown hair, wanted straight, blond hair in high school.

Artistic hair-styling frequently altered Corey's appearance. Even when Cecil didn't like Corey's hairstyles and color, he agreed we wouldn't make hair a major battlefield. The only way we limited Corey's creative hair designs was to make him pay for his hair-coloring products and haircuts.

Usually Corey stripped the color from his hair, leaving it streaked with blond or white highlights. One Christmas Eve, however, Corey emerged from the bathroom with deep-black hair. Not only was his hair black, but so were his ears and the back of his neck where the hair dye had run. Usually I could manage to say something positive about a new hairdo. This time I blew up.

"Why do you want to look so unattractive? This is the last straw. I forbid you to do anything else to your hair!" I whirled around and went into my bedroom, fighting the burning tears.

A few minutes later Corey found me furiously scrubbing the bathtub and crying.

"Mom, can we talk?" he asked tentatively.

"I don't think we have anything to talk about," I resisted, embarrassed by losing control and hurt by his action.

"Mom, please help me. I don't like it either." The anguish in his 16-year-old face told me that was true.

Later that evening, when he tried to strip out the black, his already overbleached, porous hair turned orange. His scalp burned from the dye and bleach. Every Christmas our family laughs at that story. At the time, however, this minor escalated quickly into a major.

● **Thoughtful reaction works best.** Often when a minor explodes into a major issue, there's only time for reaction, not well-thought-out action. We had another minor issue in our family develop more slowly into a major problem. This time careful planning provided a different approach.

Corey likes a wide variety of music. Early in his teenage years we tried to teach him discernment as he listened to records and tapes. Music was a minor.

In the 11th grade, however, Corey's musical tastes turned to death rock, a frightening heavy metal music with lyrics and rhythms emphasizing death and depression. The posters on his walls portrayed anger and death.

After much thought and prayer, Cecil and I confronted Corey with our concern. I explained that Corey appeared as addicted to his music as if it were a drug. We urged him to think about his involvement with this music and to evaluate its influence on him. Then we asked him to let us know what he'd do.

After our discussion I heard him call a friend to say he'd be late picking up the friend. Soon he appeared in my study.

"I don't think I'm addicted to that music. To prove it to you and Dad and myself, I've taken down all my posters and put the posters and the tapes in a box. I've decided not to listen to any death rock music for two weeks. I hope you're happy."

He was not happy, but his actions were positive. In fact he went beyond the discipline we would've used.

The death rock music event provides ideas for dealing with an escalating minor issue:

1. Identify the issue. Cecil and I were brief and focused on one issue when we talked with Corey.

2. Ask for a specific response. Because Corey is a thinker, we appealed to this characteristic by asking him to think about the situation and how he could change it.

3. Handle the problem in private. We talked in his room, away from his sister.

What were the results? At the end of his self-imposed two-week moratorium, Corey threw away his posters and sold his albums. He decided he didn't like the depression he felt when he listened to the music.

Music moved back to minor-issue status.

●　　●　　●

With clearly defined boundaries and consistency, most day-to-day issues tend to remain minor. Although teenagers press constantly against these boundaries, choose to battle over extreme violations. The rest of the time keep minors minor.

TIME OUT

1. What do you nag your teenager about? Discuss your feelings with your teenager. Ask for your teenager's feelings too. Work on ways to make this less frustrating. Try one idea at a time until you find a solution.

2. Let your teenager select two areas from the list at the beginning of this chapter where he or she would like more freedom. Evaluate your willingness to make each issue a minor.

CHAPTER**FIVE**

SET BOUNDARIES WITHOUT BUILDING BARRIERS

The party quickly jumped into full swing. Alcohol flowed freely. Couples stole into dark corners. Others disappeared briefly outside and returned with knowing smiles. It didn't take Stephanie long to decide this party was not for her. She climbed into her car and drove home.

Her mom was surprised to see Stephanie home so early.

"I didn't like the party, so I came home," Stephanie explained.

Her mom cut in, "You said you were going to Rhonda's. I didn't know you were going to a party."

"It was Rhonda's party, but I didn't think she'd let it get out of control. I didn't do anything wrong, Mom."

Stephanie's mom didn't hear her explanation. Once she heard the word "party," her anxiety level launched into orbit. "I can't believe you went to a party! Kids get into trouble at parties. Since you disobeyed me, you're grounded for two weeks."

"I didn't have to tell you about the party," Stephanie replied angrily. "I thought you'd be glad I came home instead of staying when all that stuff was going on. Next time I won't tell you anything."

"You know my rules about parties," her mother retaliated.

Stephanie tossed her dark curls defiantly. "Actually, Mom," Stephanie sighed, "No, I don't."

Stephanie's not the only teenager who doesn't know the rules established by parents. Parents either change the rules frequently or don't clearly state what they are. Even when parents identify these rules, teenagers often intentionally or unintentionally fail to hear them.

How sad that Stephanie ends her senior year with one more brick in the barrier that often separates parents and teenagers. This barrier inhibits communication by keeping parents and teenagers angry at one another.

BOUNDARIES VS. BARRIERS

Small children require barriers to protect them from harm. So parents build fences around children's play areas. As kids grow, the barriers parents construct may not be visible, but they can confine just as much. Teenagers growing toward adulthood need boundaries to guide them. How do we set these boundaries without constructing barriers that shut off a teenager from the world?

● *Boundaries define a teenager's world in terms of dos—not don'ts.* "You can talk to me about anything." "You can go to the party as long as the parents are home." "You can drive anywhere within a five-mile radius of home." Boundaries give teenagers freedom to discover what they *can* do instead of what they can't.

In contrast, barriers limit areas of life using don'ts. "Don't stay out past midnight." "Don't go to parties." "Don't raise your voice to me." "Don't get into trouble." They tend to generalize and set unreasonable expectations.

● *Boundaries establish reasons for limitations.* "I've heard the kids' new hangout isn't very safe. But you can go some other places we all agree to." No one likes to be ordered around, much less by such phrases as, "Because I'm boss," "Because I said so" or "Don't ask questions, just do as I say." When we give reasons for decisions, we communicate respect and a willingness for dialogue.

● *Parents who establish boundaries include the teenager in the process.* They willingly give a teenager choices and encourage communication. For example, if the boundary states our daughter should be home by midnight, we may offer her the choice of staying out until midnight or coming in at 11:30 p.m. and letting her friend stay until midnight.

Parents recognize that boundaries need to be flexible to adapt to the situation. On prom night, for example, we're willing to make a later curfew.

● *Setting boundaries actually lets your teenager know you care.* In his 10th grade, Corey's friend Carlos moved into an apartment in his parents' basement. Carlos came and went as he pleased. Even though Corey envied Carlos' freedom, he later admitted: "I don't think Carlos' parents care what happens to him. They never tell him what he can or can't do."

Boundaries also offer security. My mom told me and I told my kids, "Always blame me if you need an excuse to get out of something." So if I didn't want to go to a party, I'd say, "I can't go. My mom wants me to come home right after the game."

HOW BARRIERS DIVIDE

*B*oth parents and teenagers build barriers using various "bricks." Sometimes the bricks are innocently laid into place. For example, one time when I couldn't stand it anymore, I cleaned up Casey's room. In my noble quest, I gave away some of her stuffed animals I thought she didn't want anymore to a children's hospital. Unfortunately, I found out later that she still loved those animals. She's still hurt by my thoughtless act.

Other times the barriers are deliberately built. Living behind a closed bedroom door all the time while at home might be a teenager's way of hiding from the rest of the family. Let's look at some of the more common "bricks" used in building barriers.

The brick of **abusive language** usually begins by exchanging harsh words. Putdowns, inappropriate teasing and name-calling also build barriers.

The brick of **body language** gets in the way of creative discipline. Folded arms, slumped shoulders, downcast eyes say: "This is boring. I won't listen."

The brick of **inappropriate actions** quickly builds barriers. A person who storms out of the room shuts off the other person's conversation. Tears and anger are two other bricks often used in building a barrier.

The brick of **unacceptable attitudes** plays an important part in building barriers. Jealousy, fear, lack of trust, frustration, revenge and disgust are a few of the attitudes that build a wall between parents and teenagers.

HOW BOUNDARIES WORK

*P*arents can begin chipping away at these barrier bricks by recognizing and avoiding them. Here are some steps to bring down barriers and establish boundaries.

Step 1: Build on a strong foundation. The Hebrew people prepared each generation to live in the world by carefully teaching their laws and customs to the young (Deuteronomy 6:4-9).

Long before Corey drove a car, we prepared him for that freedom. As a child, we identified places where he could and couldn't play. When he started riding a bicycle, the neighborhood was his first boundary. Gradually that boundary grew along with his skills and our level of trust. Soon he could ride over to see his grandmother several miles away. Each time he left, he told us where he was going and when he'd be back.

By the time he began driving a car, Corey knew the boundaries. Of course, he complained about always having to report his actions to us. Eventually, however, he'd leave a note telling us where he was going and when he'd return if no one was available to ask him the questions.

Step 2: Learn to let go. As a young man, Jesus indicated to his parents when it was time to let go. " 'Didn't you know I had to be in my Father's house?' " he asked them in the temple courts after they'd searched all over Jerusalem. (See Luke 2:41-52 for the whole story.) Like many parents today, perhaps Jesus' parents didn't know how to let go.

A mother once asked me, "When do I start letting my teenager go?" She was almost too late. Letting go begins as soon as we recognize our children's readiness to accept responsibility.

As the parent's realm of responsibility decreases, the teenager's realm of responsibility increases. Selecting clothes, managing money, taking part-time jobs and learning to study are a few areas where parents should be able to let go gracefully.

Carefully calculated risks enhance the letting-go process. I couldn't believe it when my mom tossed me her car keys and let me drive alone to the store on the same day I obtained my driver's license.

As a mom I face the same risk next month when Casey turns 16. Although she may not be completely skilled at driving in Atlanta traffic, I'll have to let her do so sooner or later. By letting go I stroke her self-esteem and build trust. It won't be easy. Risk-taking never is.

Step 3: Specify boundaries. Parents sometimes define a boundary only when a problem arises. But it's much better for everyone to anticipate problems and communicate specific boundaries. Kids can't read minds.

Initially, we told Corey to do his best and make good grades in school. Our vague boundary meant one thing to us and another to Corey. In his freshman year at college, he interpreted "do your best" to mean C's with a few B's to offset his occasional D's.

Finally, we realized our mistake. We specifically changed the boundary from "doing your best" to "no grade lower than a C." Now there are no more problems between what we expect and the grades he earns.

Step 4: Offer choices. During the summer between Corey's junior and senior year, we tried to give him more freedom. Corey loved his independence a little too much. After several weeks of going out every night and returning home late, we gave him a choice: "Either you set the boundaries on your lifestyle, or we will. Please let us know what you plan to do by tomorrow morning."

The next morning he suggested a plan. "I think I should be allowed to go out four nights a week. I'll be home by 1 a.m." Since he worked several nights a week, we negotiated his plan down to two nights other than those he worked. For the rest of the summer the basic plan worked.

Step 5: Model consistent, acceptable behavior. Jesus invited his disciples to follow him. Then he showed them and taught them the best way to know God (John 14:9). He realized the value of a consistent example.

Teenagers learn from parents. We need to demonstrate the same courtesy and respect we desire from our teenagers. For example, be polite to a teenager's friends. And knock before entering a teenager's room.

Teenagers may not always hear what we say, but they watch what we do. Sally and Susan no longer respected their single mother's teachings about no sex outside marriage after they found her birth-control pills.

Step 6: Use positive follow-through. In the parable of the talents, Jesus told how the one who didn't use his talent was disciplined and how the two who increased their talents were rewarded (Matthew 25:14-30).

When a boundary's crossed, a teenager should expect discipline. Some parents punish. Others allow natural consequences to discipline. A few parents use their own unique methods.

I once asked the mother of three sons how she'd been so successful in rearing them. Betty credited part of her success to the support she and her husband gave their sons' activities. "I went to so many basketball games, I felt I knew the referees intimately."

Then she shared a simple discipline method she used. Whenever Betty saw one of her sons acting inappropriately she would walk by and gently tap him three times on the back. If she couldn't touch him, she'd hold up three fingers for the wayward son to see. Those three fingers or taps meant, "I love you, and I trust you to quit what you're doing and act in an acceptable way." One son told me that even when his mother wasn't around he could feel those three taps as soon as he started doing something wrong. Today her sons are a hospital administrator, the president of a bank and a minister.

Some parents identify a consequence as they set the boundary. Others don't. If the natural consequence makes the boundary clearer, then it's helpful. If stating the consequence sounds like a threat, then it's not. For example, if a teenager is about to go to a video arcade, tell him if he spends all of his allowance there, then he should expect no extra money or advance later.

Step 7: Move from external to internal controls. External controls of peers, parental limits, societal expectations and written laws set boundaries to teach people to live together in a society.

But internal controls offer strength from within (1 John 4:4). Those who set personal boundaries based on internal controls deal better with life's adventures and crises.

We believe attending worship, Sunday school and youth groups provides positive perspectives to help young Christians grow in their faith. During his senior year Corey begged to skip Sunday school. We wanted to give Corey boundaries, but I felt strongly about letting him make some decisions himself before living on his own at college. After several discussions we asked Corey to participate in Sunday school through December. After that time if he still wanted to quit he could stop going to Sunday school—but not worship service.

January came and went. Corey kept attending Sunday school. By March my curiosity got to me. I asked him why he continued coming to Sunday school.

"It's not so bad now, Mom. I decided they need me to keep everybody from settling for the Sunday school answer," he explained with a mischievous grin. I smiled, seeing a small glimpse of the man Corey was becoming.

In this process Corey moved from external restraints placed on him by us to his own internal controls. After evaluating the situation, he saw the positive contribution he could make instead of negative limits on his freedom.

WHERE BOUNDARIES HELP

*I*t's not hard to set reasonable boundaries. These basic questions can help you identify general boundary guidelines:

1. What's my teenager's need in this area?
2. What do I want from my teenager?
3. What would be the best-situation scenario?
4. What will guide my teenager toward that experience?

If you listed all your rules, it might look like a law book. Still, it's important for teenagers to know your expectations and limits. Most regulations depend on several variables.

● *Consider your teenager's age.* Younger teenagers require more structure than older teenagers. Boundaries can expand as teenagers gain competence and the trust level increases.

● *Evaluate each teenager's personality.* I'm still amazed at the wide range of personality differences among children of the same parents. Match the rule to each teenager's unique personality.

● *Finally, evaluate your level of trust formed by your teenager's past experiences.* Has your teenager been trustworthy in the past? If so, you can build on that trust by giving more responsibility. If not, your teenager may not be ready for more.

WHEN KIDS GO BEYOND THE BOUNDARIES

*E*ven when boundaries are positive, teenagers still continue to press their limits. They want to test our commitment to that boundary. They also want to test how far they can go.

It started as a simple question. "Corey, are you going out with Doug?" It stopped short of World War III. Along the way were challenges to my authority, declarations of freedom and angry statements from both sides.

These confrontations didn't happen daily, but they occurred often enough to fuel frustration. Corey wasn't a "bad kid." He just pressed hard against our boundaries.

It's a fact parents must accept: Teenagers test the rules. Even if our teenagers helped establish the boundaries, they'll push against—and sometimes break—the rules.

Most of the time this behavior springs from the normal conflict between teenagers seeking to live too soon in an adult world and parents being unwilling to let go.

Parents' expectations of what's acceptable create additional problems. Parents measure acceptable behavior by adult standards; teenagers follow norms and values set by peers.

In his junior year of high school Corey came home with a Christmas present from a friend: an earring in his ear. "How could I turn down a friend's gift, Mom? I had to do it!" (It's incredible how the teenage mind thinks sometimes.)

"The earring is unacceptable, Corey. But I'll give you a choice. You can wear your earring or drive your car."

He tried to compromise by putting a small adhesive strip over the earring. "You can hardly see it," he challenged.

When we took away his car keys, he realized we were serious. The earring came out. For a while he wore the earring when he wasn't around us. Soon the hole grew too small, and he finally gave it up.

HOW TO HANDLE BROKEN BOUNDARIES

*T*he key to dealing with broken boundaries is your reaction. If you can step away from the immediate conflict even briefly and analyze the situation, you'll deal with the problem more creatively.

● *Recognize teenagers' needs.* Are they looking for acceptance? Do they feel unworthy of your love? Teenagers often harbor unresolved hurts and disappointments. Built-up anger or resentment can cause problems too.

● *State expectations clearly.* Give clear instructions of what you want from your teenager. Eye contact ensures that your teenager is listening.

● *Send "I messages."* Saying, "You left the family room in a shambles," puts a teenager on the defensive. "I messages" focus on your feelings as the parent. "I get angry when I have to clean up after you've been in the family room. Please go pick up your trash."

Confront your teenager with the problem, but don't attack the teenager's character. Watch out for putdowns disguised as "I messages." These sound okay but really attack the teenager. "I hate it when you leave the family room in shambles."

● *Let the teenager deal with the consequences.* One special evening Corey set his curfew at 2 a.m. I was jolted awake around 2:30 a.m. and realized Corey wasn't home. When he came in at 3:15 a.m. I was reading in my study. He started to explain his lateness, but I cut him off. "It's too late to get into this now. We both know you're late. We'll discuss it in the morning." Then I went back to bed.

The next morning Corey apologized for being late. He said he had a reason, but he knew it didn't change the fact that he was late. Since he had set his own curfew and missed it, he knew he'd be disciplined. We settled on a midnight curfew for two weeks.

● *Refrain from finding fault.* Rather than playing the blame game, realize that teenagers are becoming. They'll make mistakes and so will you. Move on from there.

● *Rebuild trust.* After a boundary has been overstepped it takes time to regain the lost trust. Ask your teenager to suggest ideas for re-establishing that trust.

To re-establish trust with his parents after he came home drunk, Ron let them monitor his household chores. After three weeks of faithfully doing his chores and coming home clean, his parents decided to trust Ron again. They even quit checking up on him when he came in at night. He's been careful not to endanger that trust again.

● *Lean toward forgiveness.* Be as gracious to your teenager in forgiving past mistakes as God is in forgiving your past mistakes. After Corey's missed curfew, he wanted to go to a late movie with friends who were home from college for the holidays. So I let him stay out past midnight one of the nights he was on restriction.

Setting boundaries and maintaining trust require large doses of prayer, patience and problem-solving. Our parents used to tell us that tasks requiring lots of time and effort are the most worthwhile. This is especially true of raising children.

TIME OUT

1. Together with your teenager, list the boundaries you've established in areas of life such as school, curfew, friends, language, household chores, car use and social situations. Discuss how the rules might change as your teenager matures.

2. Write a definition of trust. Ask your teenager to do the same. Compare these definitions. Praise your teenager for the times and ways he or she has earned your trust.

CHAPTER**SIX**

❖

FAILURE IS NEVER FINAL

❖

"If babies came into the world as teenagers," Casey once mused, "people would never have children."

Casey's statement implies the struggles, difficulties, faults and failures parents experience. She quietly observed Cecil and me ranting, threatening, pleading, worrying and crying through Corey's teenage years. She sympathized with our pain but identified with his side too. How quickly her reassuring hug comforted me. How deftly her words pointed out Corey's position. Now as a teenager, she presses gently but firmly for her own independence.

Every parent faces these same struggles, disappointments and failures while guiding a teenager's transformation from awkward adolescent to acceptable adult. Sometimes these failures are real. Other times, a parent decides too early that he or she has failed, when really the teenager is still in the process of becoming. Parents shouldn't measure their failures—or their successes—too soon.

Remember how many times that child fell down as a baby before learning to walk? Adolescence is another time when kids fall down. Parents are around to help them back to their feet. Creative discipline teaches kids how to stay on their feet.

Let's not view failure as final. In fact, some forms of failure can be useful stepping stones in growth.

ACCEPTING FAILURE

*O*ne of the most intricate relationships in the Bible was between Jesus and Peter. Peter blundered through life making magnificent plans for Jesus, only to fail gravely by denying their friendship.

After the Resurrection Jesus dealt with Peter's failure at a seaside meal recorded in John 21:4-17. Parents can learn from Jesus' reaction to Peter's failure.

● *Jesus recognized that failure happened.* Jesus didn't point out Peter's denial. Instead, he addressed Peter and the other disciples as the friends they were. Jesus dealt with the present, not the past.

For some parents it's hard to face reality. Buddy's dad quickly bailed him out of jail the night Buddy was arrested for drunk driving. He excused Buddy's action by telling others, "Boys will be boys."

Unlike Buddy's father, John's parents acknowledged John's

excessive drinking. As a family they sought professional guidance. John's father explained, "We worked on John's recovery program together. After understanding why it happened, we wrote out a plan to make the future better. Each family member learned how to accept his or her limitations. We also learned how to appreciate one another."

Once acceptance replaces disappointment, the healing process begins.

● *Jesus' attitude toward Peter expressed forgiveness and hope.* Jesus encouraged Peter and the other disciples (John 21:4-8, 11). He even prepared breakfast for them (John 21:9-10, 12). As he and Peter talked, Jesus looked toward the future, pointing out Peter's major role in it (John 21:15).

Attitude makes the difference in responding to failure. If we're too proud to admit our mistakes, we're doomed to repeat them. We'll continue to talk instead of listen, to push until we're nagging, to criticize rather than affirm.

If we fear others' opinions about our teenager's failures, the correction and healing process can't start. Brenda continually bragged about her oldest son, Bobby, especially his cleverness and numerous interests. But the Bobby I knew was sullen, disruptive, destructive and clearly unhappy.

Bobby's family finally dealt with Bobby's problem after he ran away, trashed a house and overdosed on illegal drugs. In the psychiatric ward of a local hospital, Bobby asked his parents to help him overcome his drug addiction. Brenda says she failed to notice Bobby's early pleas for attention.

Bobby had to forgive his parents for their lack of attention. Brenda and her husband had to forgive Bobby's extreme rebellion. Today the family looks toward a hopeful future as they complete the final phase of Bobby's recovery.

An attitude of hope and forgiveness strengthens discipline. Forgiving parents use positive strokes in an atmosphere of encouragement, rather than constantly correcting a teenager in a climate of despair.

● *Jesus adjusted his expectations based on Peter's ability to respond.* Two times Jesus asked about Peter's love, using the ultimate word for deep, committed love (John 21:15-16). Two times Peter responded how he loved Christ, using the word for friendship. Finally, Jesus changed his expectations of love to match Peter's ability to love (John 21:17).

Parental expectations for success or failure can create unfortunate discipline demands. When a parent heaps past failures onto a teenager, that teenager's punishment may be harsher than fits the crime. Or if the teenager doesn't succeed in the manner anticipated by the parent, discipline sinks to nagging, pushing, even unreasonable pressure.

For years my high expectations for Corey's musical talent created major discipline problems. Corey played the piano as soon as he could reach the keyboard. In elementary school he won several awards with his talent. In high school he moved on to organ.

Early in his ninth-grade year, the struggle began. Corey drifted from lesson to lesson without practicing. I believed so strongly in his talent that I made this a major issue, doing all the wrong things in an effort to keep him interested. I nagged him to practice. I grounded him when he didn't. I threatened every way I could.

Finally, I adjusted my expectations of Corey. In the process of becoming, he needed space to decide who he wanted to be, not who I wanted him to be. I let him decide whether to continue his music. He stopped.

I grieved over Corey's failure (in my eyes) to continue his musical training. For Corey this "failure" opened up a new area of interest in photography and art.

For two years Corey rarely touched the piano. Now he's playing again. "But this time it's because I want to, not because I have to, Mom. It's more fun that way," he commented with a contented smile.

My expectations clashed with Corey's desires. Once I accepted who he was becoming, the tension between us diminished. I no longer felt compelled to set stringent rules in this area.

LEARNING FROM FAILURE

*A*lthough you can't always prevent failure, you can learn from it. In fact, the consequences of failure often correct inappropriate behavior quicker than punishment. As long as the teenager's health isn't damaged nor the welfare of others compromised, consequences can bring important blessings in creative discipline.

● *The blessing can be useful.* All dirty clothes in the bathroom hamper return to their owners in a wearable, clean condition. All dirty clothes outside the hamper don't. Lapses in Corey's teenage memory made him forget this longstanding maxim. After leaving towels lying on his closet floor for a week, Corey finally remembered.

"Do you know how hard it is to dry your whole body with a small hand towel?" he asked seriously as he carried the towels to the washer.

● *The blessing can be teachable.* Another longstanding rule involves morning wake-up calls. I'll wake a person one time—the rest is up to that person. Many mornings Corey yanked on jeans and a shirt as he raced to catch his 7:10 a.m. school bus.

But, alas, one day he missed it. Instead of driving him to school with a lecture on getting up on time, I let him face the consequences.

Calling friends to beg for a ride didn't work because they'd already left for school. He ended up walking the two miles to school. I wrote a note to the office explaining Corey's tardiness. He spent several afternoons in detention and caught the last bus, which let him out several blocks from home.

Corey learned to heed the clanging alarm clocks he set all over his room to get him out of bed and off to school.

● *The blessing can be painful.* Late one night I was still reading when Corey's colorless face appeared in the bedroom doorway. "Mom, I'm sorry. We didn't mean to do it," he babbled. "It wasn't our fault."

Through his terror-stricken words, I finally figured out the story. Midway through the evening Corey and his friend Doug grew bored with the teenage disco scene and decided to investigate the church graveyard across the street. Others hung out in the graveyard, but they were the only ones caught by the police. The police frisked the guys and gathered identification information. Although the police let the kids go, they warned that they'd be in touch if the church rector wanted to press charges. Corey's casual adventure had turned into a nightmare.

We talked about damaging another's property and about the sanctity of graveyards. At the time, several graveyards in the city had been trashed by teenagers who also used them in satanic rituals. "Doug and I were just walking around. We weren't looking for any trouble," he pleaded.

The police never called. But the next day Corey and I went to the graveyard and picked up the bottles and debris. Why did I go? I wanted Corey to know that I believed his story of innocence and supported his efforts in dealing with the situation.

Corey's painful lesson taught him that being in the wrong place at the wrong time could have unexpected consequences.

● ***The blessing can produce a strong reminder.*** Jimmy was already on restriction when he went to bed early one night. As his parents Austin and Sharon turned in, Austin checked on Jimmy. Instead of finding Jimmy in bed, Austin found an open window leading to the carport roof. Austin closed and locked the window and returned downstairs to wait for Jimmy to come home.

When Jimmy arrived, he climbed on the carport roof, but couldn't budge the locked window. With no other choice Jimmy used his key to come in through the front door. Neither Sharon nor Austin remembers the punishment. But they vividly remember Jimmy's surprised face when he saw his parents and knew he'd been caught.

● ***The blessing can be adaptable.*** Sandra became pregnant in 10th grade. This beautiful, bright young woman who attended a Christian high school lived with the consequences of

*"Well, I guess this is the end of life as
we know it."*

her sin. With the love and support of her parents, she gave up her baby for adoption.

Sandra adapted her failure into a powerful personal testimony, warning other teenagers about sex outside of marriage. Throughout her senior year, Sandra talked openly about her failure and its consequences.

One day Sandra spoke in chapel, expressing her reasons for giving up her baby. Casey heard this birth mother say, "I wanted a real home for my daughter, one that's better than anything I could give her." For the first time, Casey grasped how tough it had been for another birth mother to give up her tiny baby daughter.

Casey is adopted, as is Corey.

CONTROLLING FAILURE

O kay, so failure happens—to both parents and teenagers. While we may be willing to accept it, and although good can develop from the consequences, creative discipline gives ways to keep failure from being final.

● *Unconditional love*—What a powerful model the Bible presents in the unconditional, accepting love of Jesus. His unique love led Zacchaeus to see his wrong deeds as a tax collector (Luke 19:1-10). Jesus' perceptive love cut through the excuses of those who wavered in following him (Luke 9:57-62). Jesus' ability to love the person and not the action brought out the goodness in the woman who'd lived a sinful life (Luke 7:36-50).

In the day-to-day discipline of a developing young person, parents' unconditional love undergoes severe testing. How can parents love teenagers they sometimes don't even like? A teenager's selfishness and thoughtlessness can rip apart any parent's patient resolve! That's the wonder of unconditional love. Even when parents can't love using their human hearts and minds, they can allow God to love through them.

After a particularly trying week of emotional ups and downs and endless verbal skirmishes, Corey sat at the dinner table trying to apologize. "I'm sorry I've been so difficult this week. Sometimes I don't know why I do things. But no matter what I do, I know you and Dad will always love me."

Some parents live a lifetime without hearing those words of trust from their teenagers. At the time, however, the only thought that sprang to my mind (but not my mouth) was, "Don't press your luck!"

But I secretly rejoiced that he felt true security from our stumbling efforts at unconditional love.

● *Gracious forgiveness*—Galatians 6:2 compels us to "carry each other's burdens, and in this way you will fulfill the law of Christ." Few are more burdened than an anxious teenager frantically searching for identity. Yet parents often show more graciousness to strangers or casual friends than to their own children.

Grace in discipline extends support and assurance even when undeserved. Unfortunately, parents tend to measure future behavior by past mistakes. Gracious discipline doesn't hold grudges. Gracious discipline doesn't tally failures. Gracious discipline forgives and forgets. If we parents take time to understand the burdens our teenagers carry, we'll provide supportive discipline instead of criticism and faultfinding.

A PARENT'S REPORT CARD ON UNCONDITIONAL LOVE

Unconditional love lays the foundation for all discipline. It forces us to go on, even if we don't see a daily change in our teenager. Read 1 Corinthians 13, focusing on verses 4 through 8. Match the definition with Paul's words. Then grade yourself, using A through F, on your level of unconditional love.

Definition	Characteristic	Your Grade
1. _____	"Love is patient,	
2. _____	love is kind.	
3. _____	It does not envy,	
4. _____	it does not boast,	
	it is not proud.	
5. _____	It is not rude,	
6. _____	it is not self-seeking,	
7. _____	it is not easily angered,	
8. _____	it keeps no record of wrongs.	
9. _____	Love does not delight in evil	
	but rejoices with the truth.	
10. _____	It always protects,	
11. _____	always trusts,	
12. _____	always hopes,	
13. _____	always perseveres.	
14. _____	Love never fails."	

continued

Definitions

a. has faith in others; seeks a person's highest good

b. doesn't emphasize personal virtues because of an inflated ego

c. continuous; cannot be defeated

d. spontaneously gracious to others with no thought of personal reward

e. doesn't intentionally seek to hurt another

f. doesn't celebrate others' failures, but delights in goodness

g. remains strong under stress

h. supports another even in times of disappointment, frustration or indifference

i. doesn't envy another's abilities and opportunities

j. is concerned with others, rather than self

k. forgets another's past mistakes

l. doesn't want to make life miserable for others

m. is able to last even in the most difficult circumstances

n. knows God is in control; waits for God's timing

How'd you do? The correct match-ups are: 1.g; 2.d; 3.i; 4.b; 5.e; 6.j; 7.l; 8.k; 9.f; 10.h; 11.a; 12.n; 13.m; 14.c.

● *Trust*—At the other side of forgiveness lies trust. Some parents declare, "My teenager must earn my trust." Yet, how can teenagers earn trust unless opportunities give them chances to be trustworthy? To me trust must be given freely, not naively—but with expectations of the best, not the worst.

Yes, failure damages trust. But that's when trust and forgiveness must work together. If a parent's goal is to build a teenager's self-esteem, then trust—like forgiveness—must be extended again and again.

I've never heard a teenager complain, "My parents trust me too much." They usually remark, "I wish my folks would trust me more."

● *Heal the hurt*—When failure occurs, work toward healing using these steps:

1. Accept the reality of failure, then move on.

2. Discover why the failure occurred. Was the failure yours or your teenager's? What need of your teenager was being ignored?

Bobby did drugs to gain his parents' unfocused attention. Was the home environment too rigid or too lax? Did an event such as divorce or chronic illness cause the problem?

3. Work toward a solution. Use the different discipline methods discussed in this book. Keep trying until you find one that works.

4. Include your teenager in the discovery process.

While there are no easy answers, don't let failure be final.

During his senior year Bill moved from his dad's house into a friend's home. Bill's father, Bruce, viewed the act as rebellious. Actually Bill grabbed the only chance he saw to get his life together. Numerous problems at home forced Bill out, including an alcoholic parent. Over the past two years, Bruce and Bill have talked and healed many of the wounds between them. Bruce no longer sees the situation as a failure, even though Bill hasn't moved back home.

FACING THE FUTURE

"*T*rain a child in the way he should go, and when he is old he will not turn from it." This familiar verse from Proverbs 22:6 is often quoted and much misunderstood. Training begins early and continues while the child is with the parent. Parents can't rush to judgment. For "when he is old" doesn't designate the age to measure the results of that training. The discipline you teach today may not be applied until that teenager is much older.

Remember your teenager is becoming. In another 10 or 15 years, you'll probably marvel at the adult your teenager has become. You won't be able to accept all the blame for what that young adult does wrong. Neither will you take credit for all he or she does right.

While you're in the process of training, you may question your abilities and effectiveness. I always said I'd write a book called *How I Survived My Teenager*. A year ago, however, I hadn't survived Corey. Those painful episodes now stir memories, softened by time. I can laugh at the words and actions brought about by the unusual reasoning of a normal teenager.

Today I view those experiences through the bright window of hope. I've seen Corey's future, and it promises the mature, reasonable adult I knew he could become. I even think I'll make it through the rest of Casey's adolescent years.

Oh, I'm no Alice in Wonderland. I realize the grave dangers and incredible pressures our teenagers face. I've not addressed the way to discipline many major problems such as drug abuse, runaways, homosexuality or sexual promiscuity. Experts write complete books on each of these topics.

Instead, I've tried to encourage you to examine new ways to approach daily discipline. As you've read this book, perhaps you've evaluated your own discipline methods.

The **substance** of creative discipline builds on a willingness to try effective ways to guide and correct your teenager's attitude and behavior.

The **strength** of creative discipline comes from a relationship established early, grounded in mutual trust and forged with healthy communication.

The **secret** of creative discipline emphasizes more pluses than minuses in evaluating your teenager's behavior, negotiating boundaries, reacting to problems and assessing your attitude.

The **success** of creative discipline can be recognized if you don't judge too early. Rejoice in what God can do through your efforts and your failures.

"Weeping may remain for a night, but rejoicing comes in the morning" (Psalm 30:5b).

Whether you stagger through the black night of a teenager's fluctuating moods and behaviors, or glimpse the shimmering dawn of hope ahead, know that joy comes in guiding your teenager. And remember—you're not alone!

TIME OUT

1. What "failure" most disturbs you? Was it yours or your teenager's? After reading this chapter, what can you do to heal the hurt?

2. Sometimes we don't know how we've failed others. Share with your teenager times when you feel you failed. Ask your teenager to tell you about times when you failed and didn't realize it. Ask for forgiveness. Pray with your teenager, asking for God's forgiveness also.